Basic Instructions

Paper: The best paper to use for traditional origami is very thin, keeps a crease well, and folds flat. You can use plain white paper (good for learning), solid-color paper, or wrapping paper with a design only on one side. Be aware, though, that some kinds of paper stretch slightly, either in length or in width, while others tear easily.

Packets of papers especially for use in origami (15 by 15 centimeters square, or about 6 by 6 inches) are available in a variety of colors from craft and hobby shops. They may also carry origami paper in a larger size. You can, however, easily square off rectangular sheets.

Regular typing paper may be too heavy to allow for the many tight folds needed in creating more complex, traditional origami figures, but it should be fine for several of the larger papercraft works, with fewer folds, given here. For those who are learning, and have a problem getting their fingers to work tight folds, larger paper sizes are fine. Slightly larger figures are easier to make than overly small ones.

Glue: Use a good, easy-flowing but not loose paper glue, but use it sparingly. You don't want to soak the paper. A flat toothpick makes a good applicator. Apply glue as needed then allow the glued form time to dry. Avoid using stick glue, as the application pressure needed (especially if the stick has become dry) can damage your figure.

Technique: Fold with care. Position the paper, especially at corners, precisely and see that edges line up before creasing a fold. Once you are sure of the fold, use a fingernail to make a clean, flat crease. Don't get discouraged with your first efforts. In time, what your mind can create, your fingers can fashion.

Symbols & Lines

Fold lines	valley		Fold then unfold		
	mountain				
Cut line			Pleat fold (repeated folding)		
Turn over or rotate			Crease line		

1

Basic Folds

Kite Fold

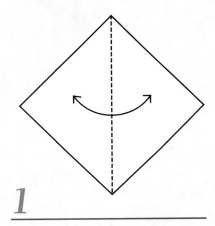

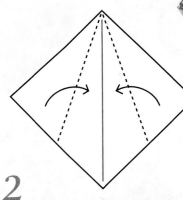

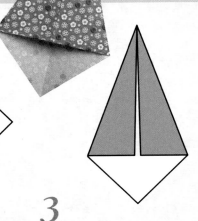

1

Fold and unfold a square diagonally, making a center crease.

2

Fold both sides in to the center crease.

3

This is a kite form.

Valley Fold ----------------

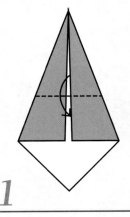

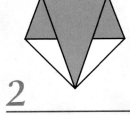

1

Here, using the kite, fold form toward you (forward), making a "valley."

2

This fold forward is a valley fold.

Mountain Fold —·—·—·—·—·—·—·—

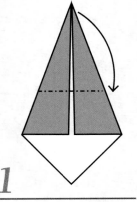

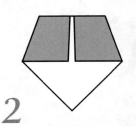

1

Here, using the kite, fold form away from you (backwards), making a "mountain."

2

This fold backwards is a mountain fold.

Inside Reverse Fold

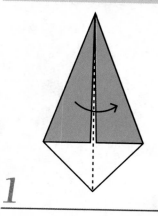

1
Starting here with a kite, valley fold kite closed.

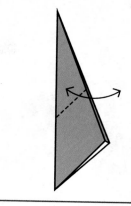

2
Valley fold as marked to crease, then unfold.

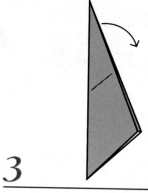

3
Pull tip in direction of arrow.

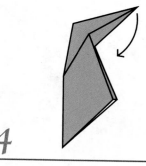

4
Appearance before completion.

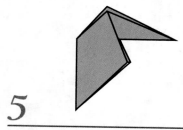

5
You've made an inside reverse fold.

Outside Reverse Fold

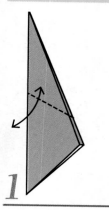

1
Using closed kite, valley fold, unfold.

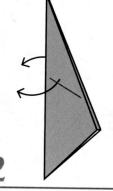

2
Fold inside out, as shown by arrows.

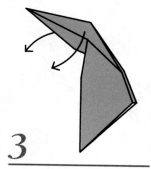

3
Appearance before completion.

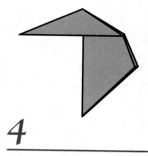

4
You've made an outside reverse fold.

Basic Folds

Pleat Fold

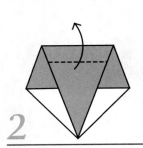

1

Here, using the kite, valley fold.

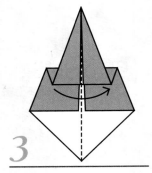

2

Valley fold back again.

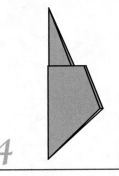

3

This is a pleat. Valley fold in half.

4

You've made a pleat fold.

Pleat Fold Reverse

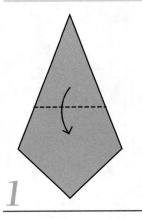

1

Here, using the kite form backwards, valley fold.

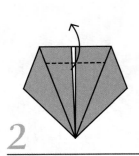

2

Valley fold back again for pleat.

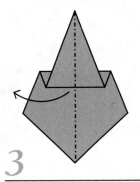

3

Mountain fold form in half.

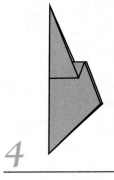

4

This is a pleat fold reverse.

Squash Fold I

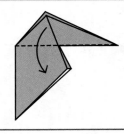

1

Using inside reverse, valley fold one side.

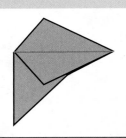

2

This is a squash fold I.

Squash Fold II

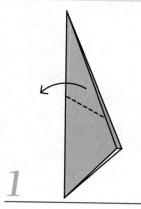

1

Using closed kite form, valley fold.

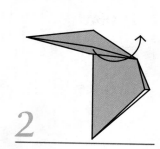

2

Open in direction of the arrow.

3

Appearance before completion.

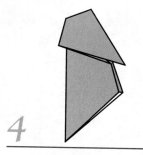

4

You've made a squash fold II.

Inside Crimp Fold

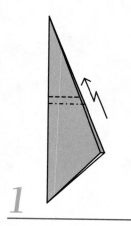

1

Here, using closed kite form, pleat fold.

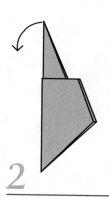

2

Pull tip in direction of the arrow.

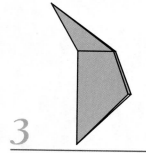

3

This is an inside crimp fold.

Outside Crimp Fold

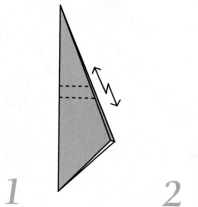

1

Here, using closed kite form, pleat fold and unfold.

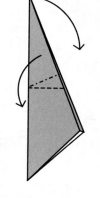

2

Fold mountain and valley as shown, both sides.

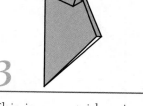

3

This is an outside crimp fold.

Basic Folds

Base Folds

Base folds are basic forms that do not in themselves produce origami, but serve as a basis, or jumping-off point, for a number of creative origami figures, some quite complex. As when beginning other crafts, learning to fold these base folds is not the most exciting part of origami. They are, however, easy to do, and will help you with your technique. They also quickly become rote, so much so that you can do many using different-colored papers while you are watching television or your mind is elsewhere. With completed base folds handy, if you want to quickly work up a form or are suddenly inspired with an idea for an original, unique figure, you can select an appropriate base fold and swiftly bring a new creation to life.

Base Fold I

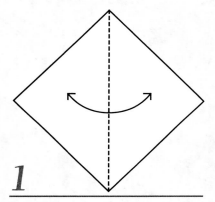

1
Fold and unfold in direction of arrow.

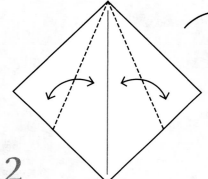

2
Fold both sides in to center crease, then unfold. Rotate.

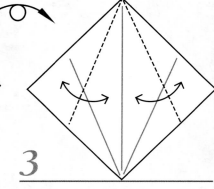

3
Fold both sides in to center crease, then unfold.

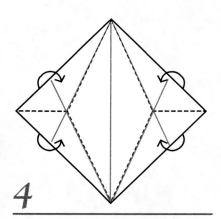

4
Pinch corners of square together and fold inward.

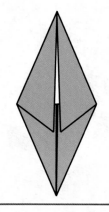

5
Completed Base Fold I.

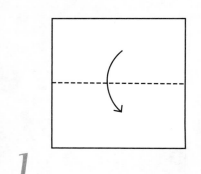

1

Valley fold.

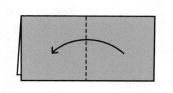

2

Valley fold.

3

Squash fold.

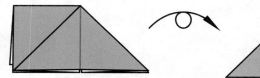

4

Turn over to other side.

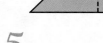

5

Squash fold.

6

Completed Base Fold II.

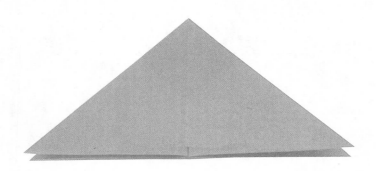

Base Folds

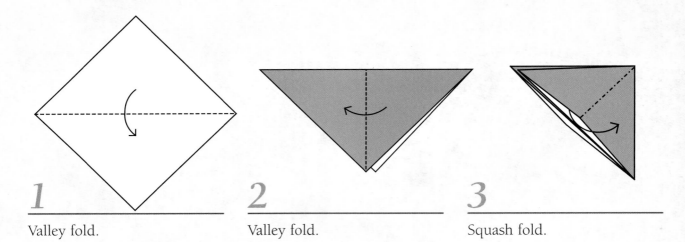

1 Valley fold.

2 Valley fold.

3 Squash fold.

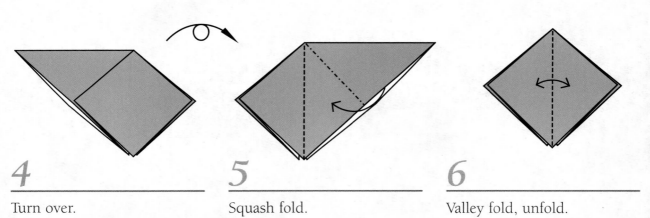

4 Turn over.

5 Squash fold.

6 Valley fold, unfold.

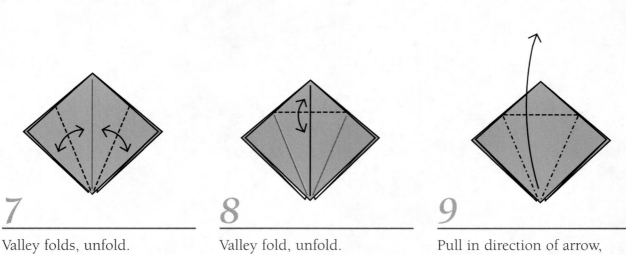

7 Valley folds, unfold.

8 Valley fold, unfold.

9 Pull in direction of arrow, folding inward at sides.

Base Folds

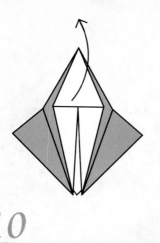

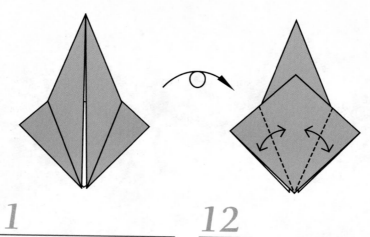

10

Appearance before
completion of fold.

11

Fold completed. Turn over.

12

Valley folds, unfold.

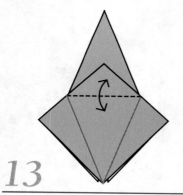

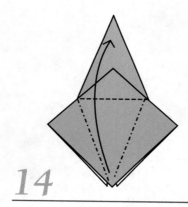

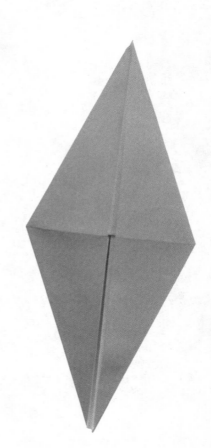

13

Valley fold, unfold.

14

Repeat, again pulling in
direction of arrow.

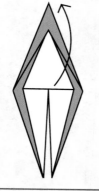

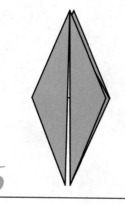

15

Appearance before
completion.

16

Completed Base Fold III.

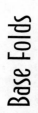

Base Folds

9

Angel

Paper Usage page 13.

Part 1

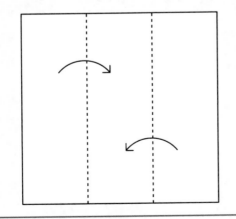

1

Valley fold sheet as shown, in thirds.

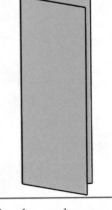

2

Apply glue to lower inside front layer only.

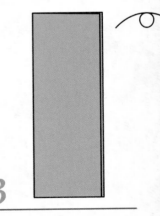

3

Turn over.

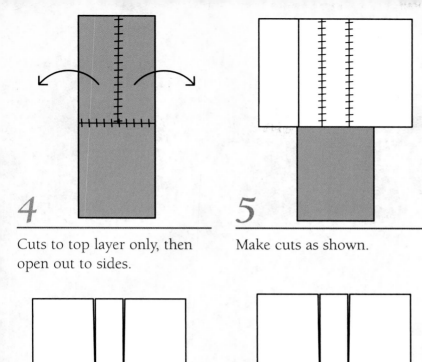

4
Cuts to top layer only, then open out to sides.

5
Make cuts as shown.

6
Cut and remove top strip. Make side cuts through.

7
Valley fold side sections.

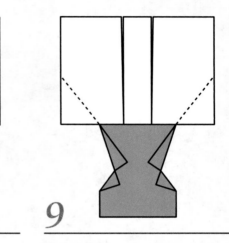

8
Apply glue to side folds.

9
Valley folds.

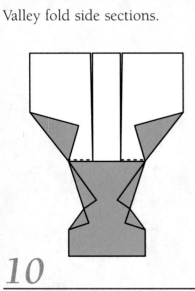

10
Valley folds.

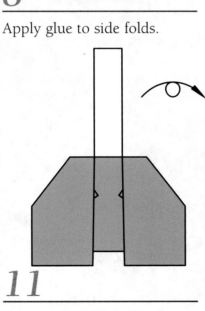

11
Turn over to other side.

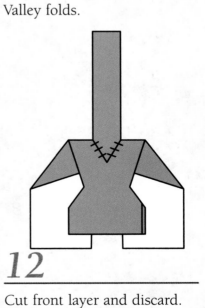

12
Cut front layer and discard.

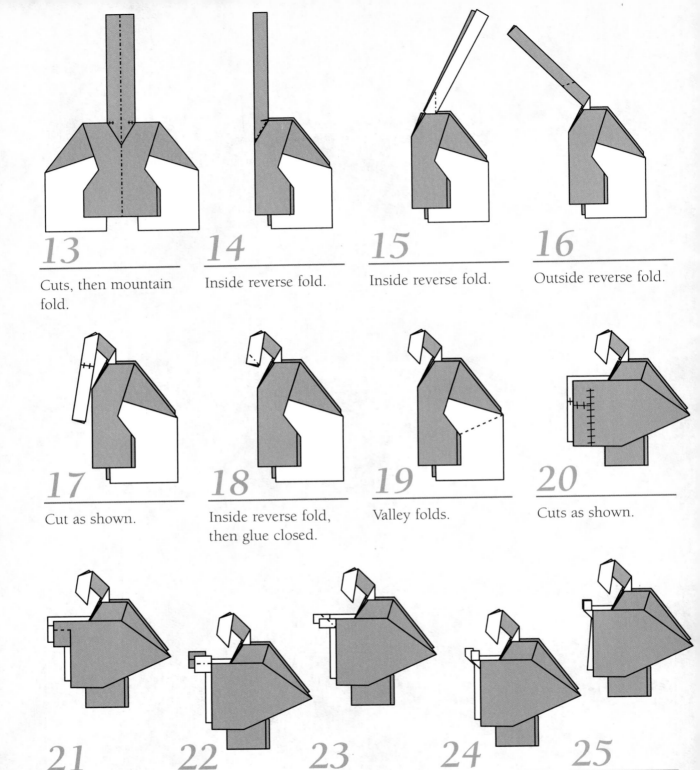

13 Cuts, then mountain fold.

14 Inside reverse fold.

15 Inside reverse fold.

16 Outside reverse fold.

17 Cut as shown.

18 Inside reverse fold, then glue closed.

19 Valley folds.

20 Cuts as shown.

21 Valley folds.

22 Mountain folds.

23 Mountain folds.

24 Glue hands together.

25 Completed part 1 (top) of angel.

Part 2

1

Roll into tube shape to fit inside angel top, and glue.

2

Cuts as shown.

3

Taper both sides and glue.

4

Completed part 2 (lower body) of angel.

Part 3

1

Valley fold strip.

2

Valley fold.

3

Inside reverse fold.

4

Cut off as shown.

5

Completed part 3 (hair) of angel.

Paper Usage

1 sheet
8.5" by 8.5"

Part 1
(top body)

1 sheet
2" by 6"

Part 3
(hair)

1 sheet
8.5" by 5"

Part 2
(lower body)

1 sheet
4" by 12"

Part 4
(wings)

Angel

13

1

Start with strip of paper, valley fold.

2

Valley fold, then rotate.

3

Valley fold.

4

Squash fold.

5

Mountain fold.

6

Cut as shown.

7

Valley fold both sides.

8

Valley fold both sides.

9

Cuts as shown.

10

Unfold, to open out wings.

11

Make cuts.

12

Completed part 4 (wings) of angel.

Angel

14

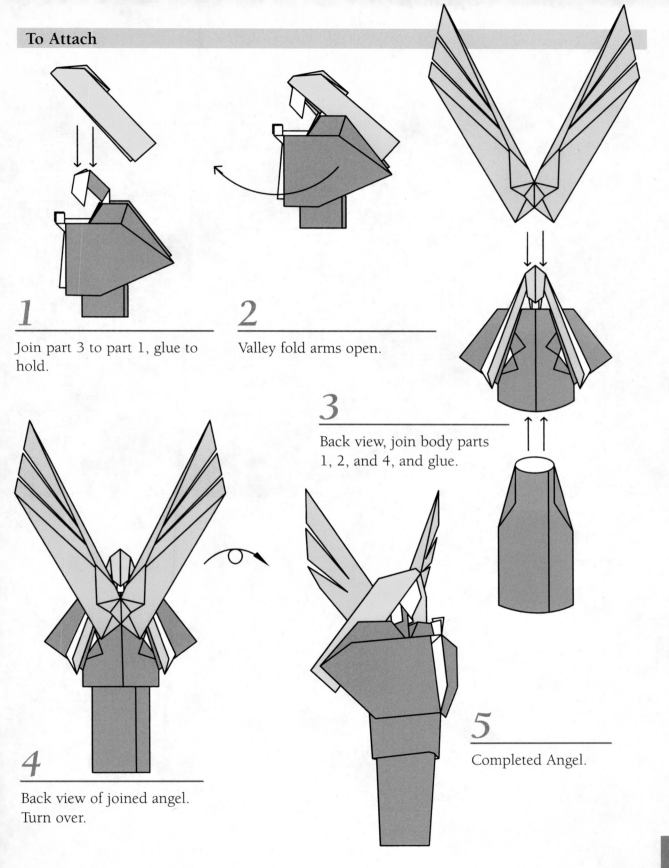

1

Join part 3 to part 1, glue to hold.

2

Valley fold arms open.

3

Back view, join body parts 1, 2, and 4, and glue.

4

Back view of joined angel. Turn over.

5

Completed Angel.

Snowman

Part 1

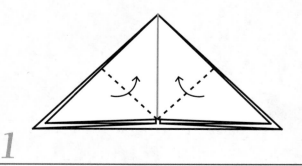

1

Using Base Fold II, valley fold sides to center crease.

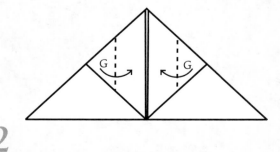

2

Apply glue (G) to triangles, then valley fold.

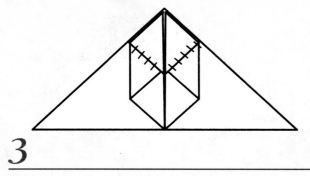

3

Make cuts to top layer as shown, and discard the two upper triangles.

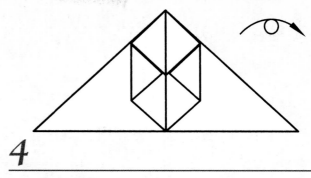

4

Turn over to other side.

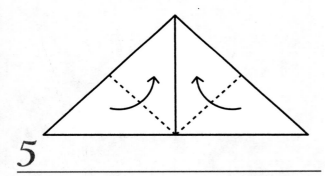

5

Again, valley folds to center crease.

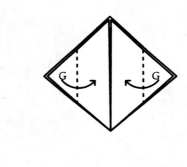

6

Apply glue, then valley fold.

7

Make cuts to the top layer and discard triangles.

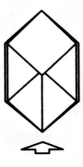

8

Blow into bottom center opening and pull form open, to inflate and form box.

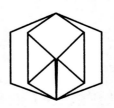

9

Part 1 (bottom body) of snowman.

Parts 2 and 3

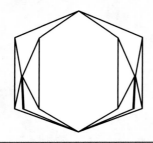

1

For part 2 (top body), make part 1 in smaller size.

2

For part 3 (head), make part 1 in even smaller size.

Part 4

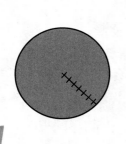 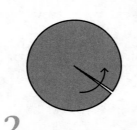 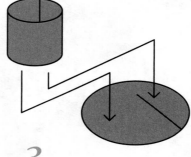 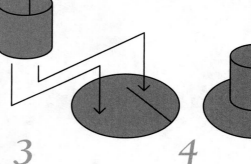

1

Make paper circle and cut as shown.

2

Pull as shown and apply glue to hold brim.

3

Form paper tube, add glue to edge and attach to brim.

4

Completed part 4 (hat) of snowman.

Part 5

 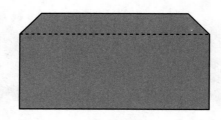 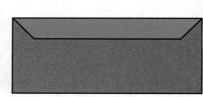

1

Start with rectangle of paper, make cuts as shown.

2

Valley fold.

3

Completed part 5 (cape) of snowman.

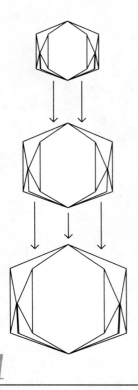

1

Build snowman,
gluing parts 1, 2, and
3 together to hold.

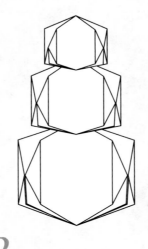

2

Basic snowman ready
for hat and cape.

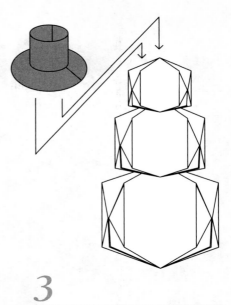

3

Glue hat to head
of snowman.

4

Wrap cape around snowman.
Glue at top corners, inside
collar, to hold.

5

Completed basic
Snowman. Add
paper-coal eyes,
carrot nose, and
mouth.

Other decoration
ideas: corncob pipe,
scarf, buttons, bow tie.

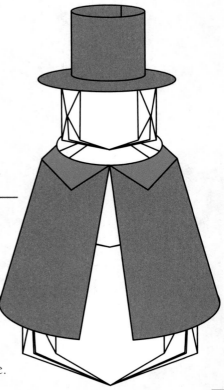

Snowman

19

Kris Kringle

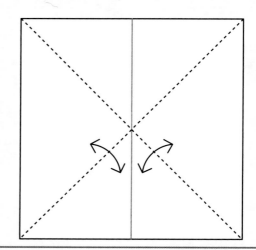

Paper Usage page 27.

Part 1

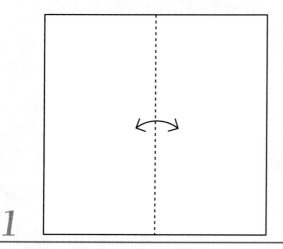

1

Valley fold then unfold.

2

Valley folds then unfold.

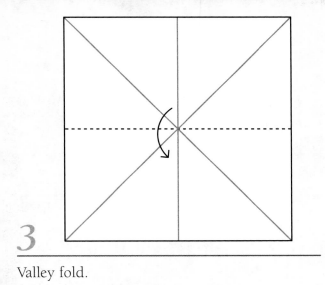

3

Valley fold.

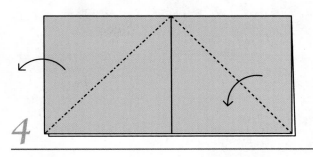

4

Mountain and valley fold.

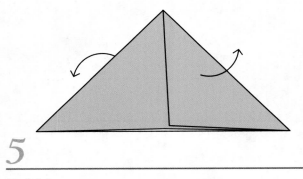

5

Unfolds.

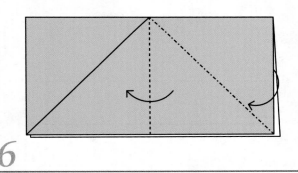

6

Squash fold.

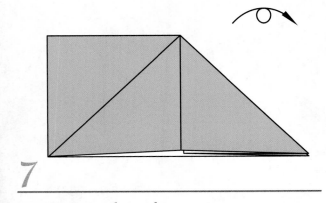

7

Turn over to other side.

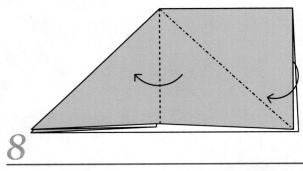

8

Squash fold.

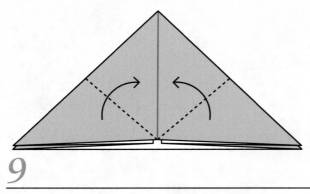

9

This is Base Fold II; now, valley folds.

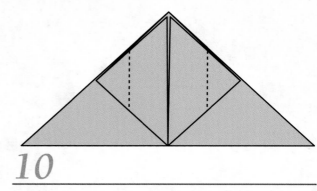

10

Valley folds.

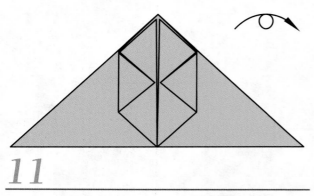

11

Turn over to other side.

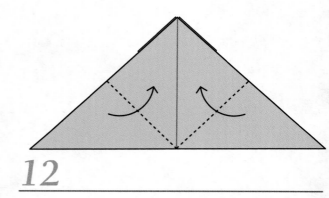

12

Valley folds.

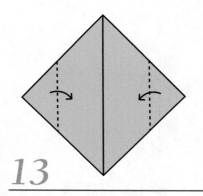

13

Valley folds.

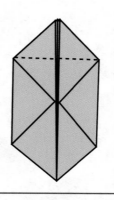

14

Valley folds, front and back.

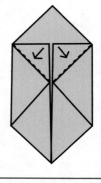

15

Valley and unfold, then tuck flaps into pockets as shown, front and back.

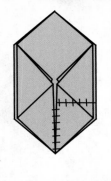

16

Cut through layers as shown.

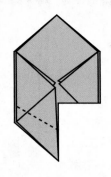

17

Outside reverse fold, both sides.

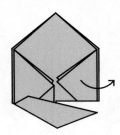

18

Unfold both sides.

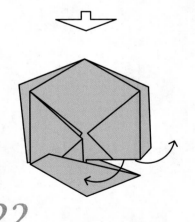

19

Cut through as shown.

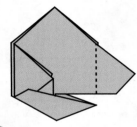

20

Valley fold and glue both sides to hold.

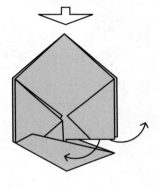

21

Push top down and open out.

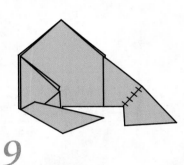

22

Appearance before completion.

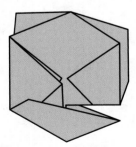

23

Completed part 1 (head) of Kris Kringle.

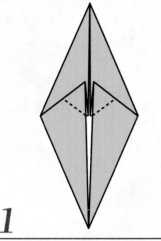

1

Start with Base Fold I, then valley folds.

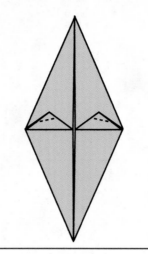

2

Inside reverse folds.

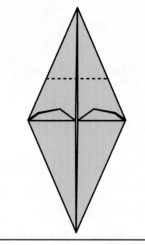

3

Valley fold.

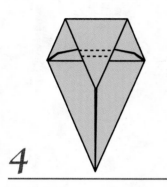

4

Pleat fold.

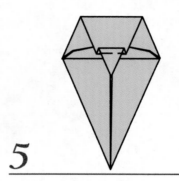

5

Valley fold.

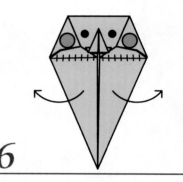

6

Draw eyes and cheeks, then cut and unfold.

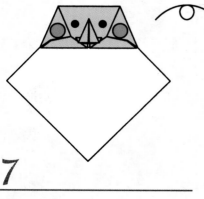

7

Turn over.

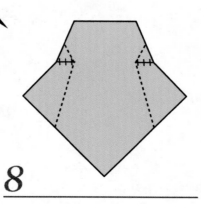

8

Cuts, then valley folds.

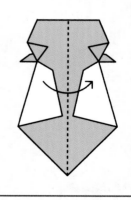

9

Valley fold in half.

Kris Kringle

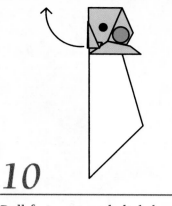

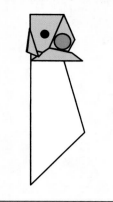

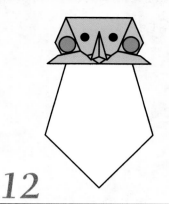

10

Pull face outward slightly
and squash fold.

11

Open out.

12

Completed part 2 (face) of
Kris Kringle.

Part 3

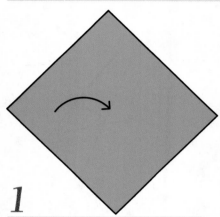

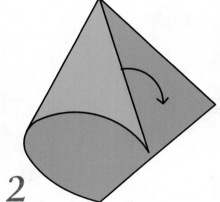

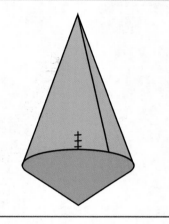

1

Roll corner of square sheet
in direction of arrow.

2

Form into cone and glue
to hold.

3

Cut as shown.

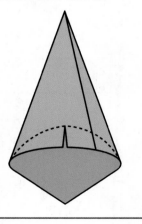

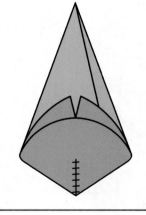

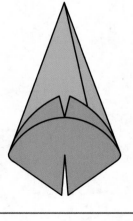

4

Valley folds.

5

Cut as shown.

6

Completed part 3 (hat) of
Kris Kringle.

Kris Kringle

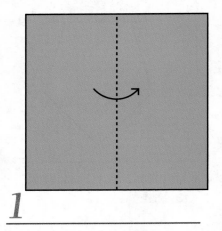

Part 4

1

Valley fold in half.

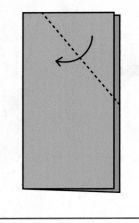

2

Valley fold layers together
and apply glue to hold.

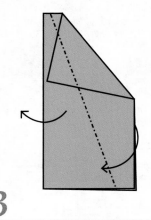

3

Open form and squash fold.

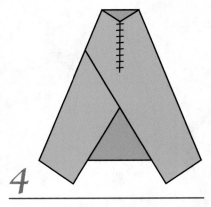

4

Cut top layer only, and
return to previous position.

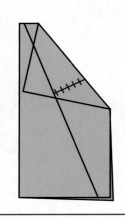

5

Cut through as shown.

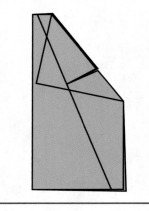

6

Squash fold open again.

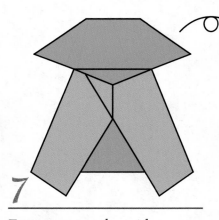

7

Turn over to other side.

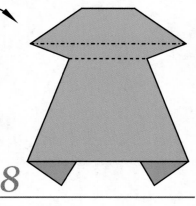

8

Pleat fold.

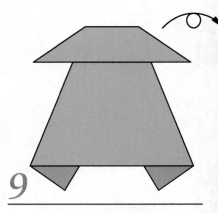

9

Turn over to other side.

Kris Kringle

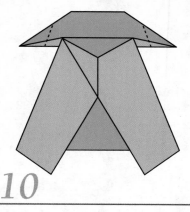

10

Valley folds, tucking flaps behind form.

11

Squash fold to side view.

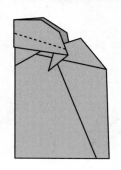

12

Outside reverse fold.

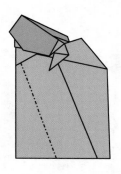

13

Inside reverse fold.

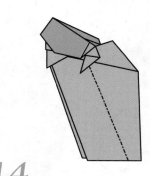

14

Squash fold to front view.

15

Complete part 4 (top body) of Kris Kringle.

Paper Usage

1 sheet
5.5" by 5.5"

Part 1 (head)

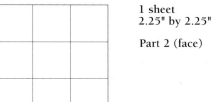

1 sheet
2.25" by 2.25"

Part 2 (face)

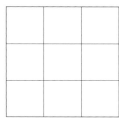

1 sheet
4.25" by 4.25"

Part 3 (hat)

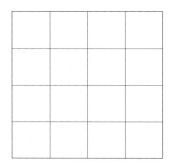

2 sheets   Part 4 (robe)
8.5" by 8.5"   Part 5 (body)

Kris Kringle

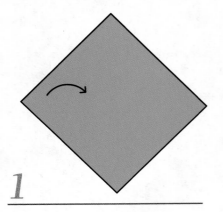

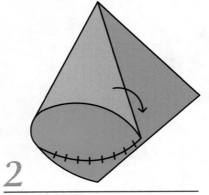

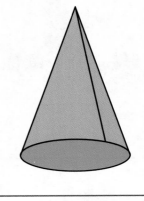

Part 5

1

Roll square sheet in direction of arrow.

2

Form into cone, glue to hold. Cut off excess.

3

Completed part 5 (body base) of Kris Kringle.

To Attach

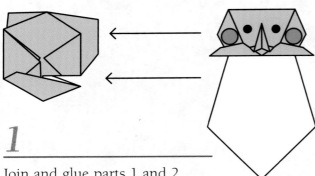

1

Join and glue parts 1 and 2 (head) together as shown.

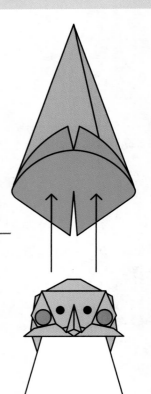

2

Add part 3 (hat) and glue to hold.

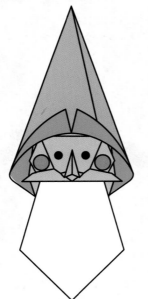

3

Completed head of Kris Kringle.

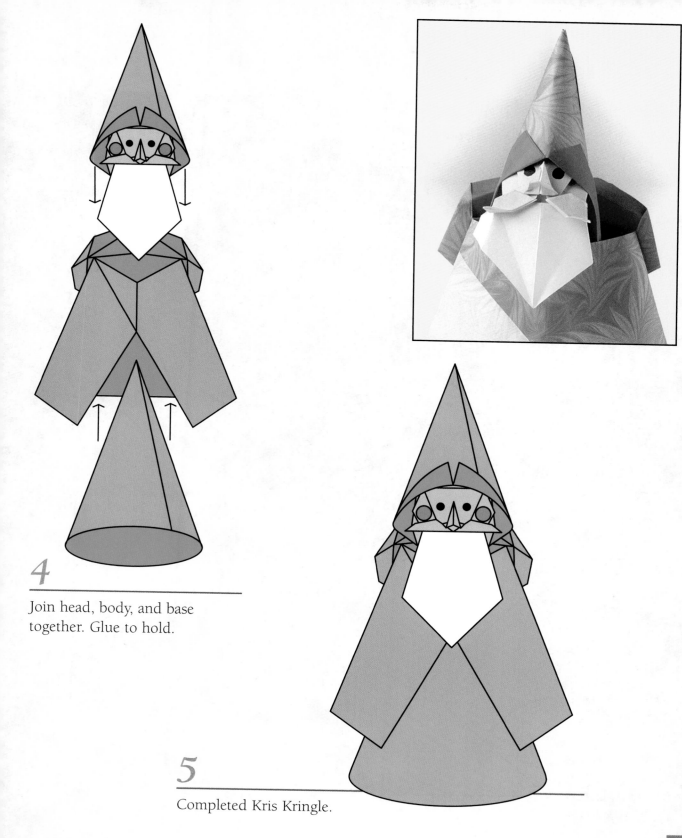

4

Join head, body, and base together. Glue to hold.

5

Completed Kris Kringle.

Santa Claus

Paper Usage page 35.

Part 1

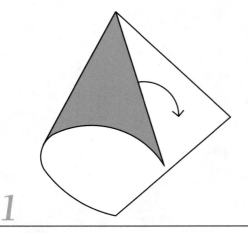

1

Roll square into cone, and glue.

2.

Cut off excess.

3

Top part of hat.

4

Start with paper strip, valley fold.

5

Fit opening of folded strip over cone end (see next step).

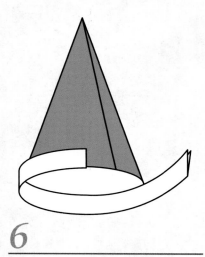

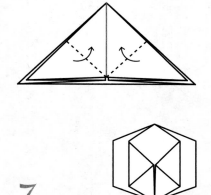

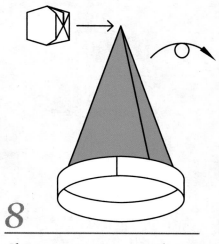

6

Wrap completely around cone end. Apply glue as you go.

7

Using small size Base Fold II, form pompom (see snowman pages 16–17).

8

Glue pompom to one side of tip of hat. Rotate.

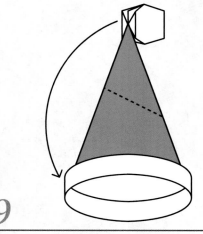

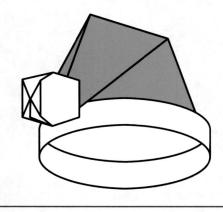

9

Valley fold to one side as shown, glue to hold pompom in position.

10

Completed part 1 (hat) of Santa Claus. (A large-sized hat makes a cute decoration in itself!)

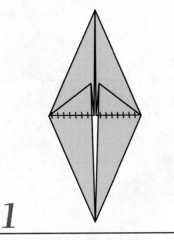

1

Start with Base Fold I, cut top layer only as shown.

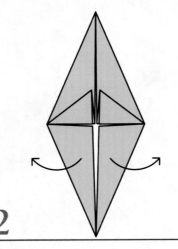

2

Unfolds.

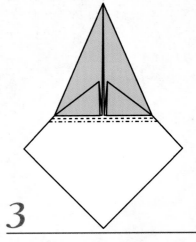

3

Pleat fold.

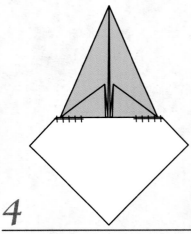

4

Cuts as shown.

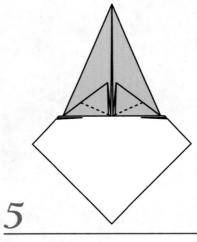

5

Valley folds.

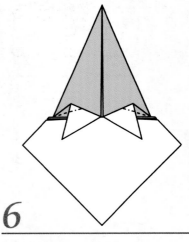

6

Inside reverse folds.

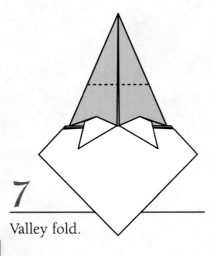

7

Valley fold.

8

Pleat fold.

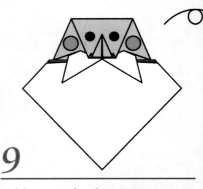

9

Add eyes, cheeks. Turn over.

Santa Claus

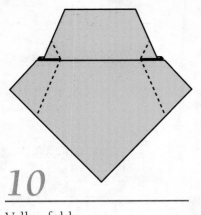

10

Valley folds.

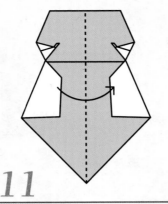

11

Valley fold in half.

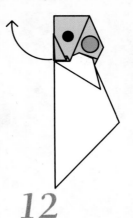

12

Pull and crimp fold.

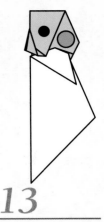

13

Valley unfold.

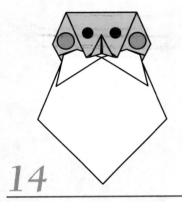

14

Tuck face section behind mustache.

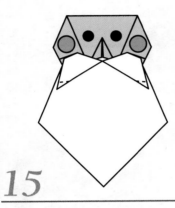

15

Valley folds.

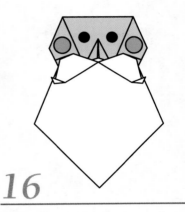

16

Completed face section, for head.

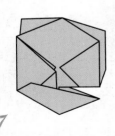

17

Make head from new square (see Kris Kringle, pages 20–23).

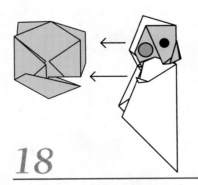

18

Attach Santa face to head.

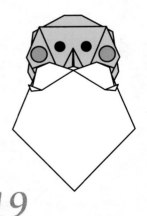

19

Completed part 2 (head) of Santa Claus.

Santa Claus

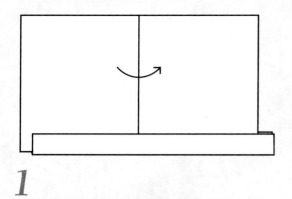

Part 3

1

Valley fold strip to fit over sheet as shown, valley fold in half.

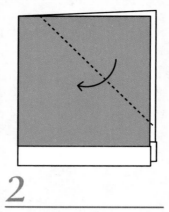

2

Valley fold both layers.

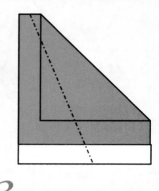

3

Glue and squash fold to open out front.

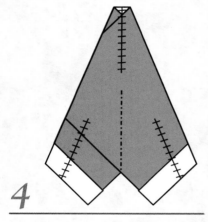

4

Cut as shown, then return to step 3 position.

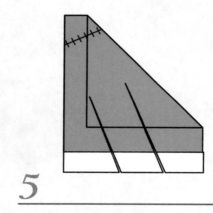

5

Cut off section as shown.

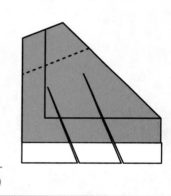

6

Valley folds both sides.

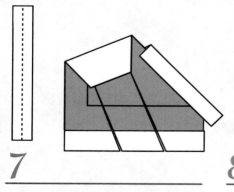

7

Trim strip length. Valley fold then glue. Squash fold.

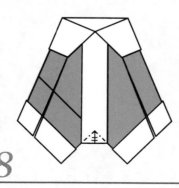

8

Cut and mountain folds.

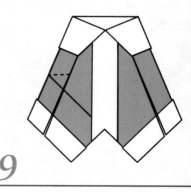

9

Valley fold arm.

Santa Claus

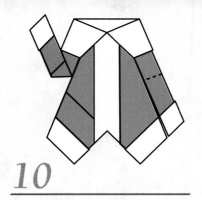

10

Valley fold other arm.

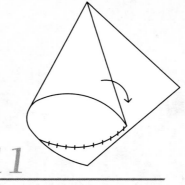

11

Roll a new sheet into cone. Glue and cut off excess.

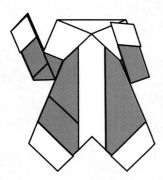

12

Insert cone into Santa's robe for better stability. Glue to hold.

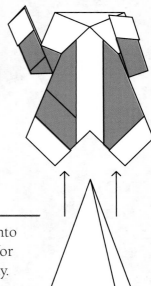

13

Completed part 3 (body) of Santa. (Liner hidden.)

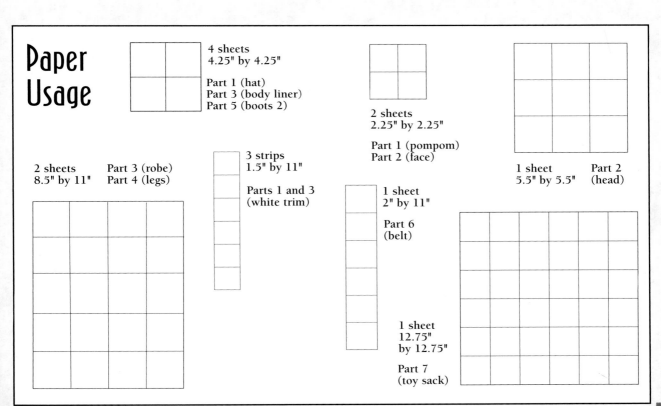

Paper Usage

4 sheets
4.25" by 4.25"

Part 1 (hat)
Part 3 (body liner)
Part 5 (boots 2)

2 sheets
2.25" by 2.25"

Part 1 (pompom)
Part 2 (face)

1 sheet
5.5" by 5.5"   Part 2 (head)

2 sheets   Part 3 (robe)
8.5" by 11"   Part 4 (legs)

3 strips
1.5" by 11"

Parts 1 and 3
(white trim)

1 sheet
2" by 11"

Part 6
(belt)

1 sheet
12.75" by 12.75"

Part 7
(toy sack)

Santa Claus

Part 4

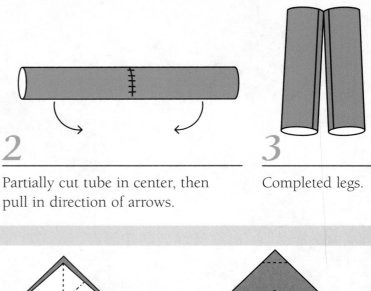

1
Roll rectangular sheet lengthwise into tube, and glue to hold.

2
Partially cut tube in center, then pull in direction of arrows.

3
Completed legs.

Part 5

1
Valley fold.

2
Pinch top layer together, mountain fold as shown.

3
Mountain fold, then valley folds.

4
Valley folds.

5
Pull together as shown and glue to hold.

6
Completed part 5 (boot) of Santa. Now repeat (make 2).

Part 6

1
Strip of paper, valley fold in thirds.

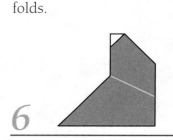

2
Cut top layer as shown, then mountain fold flap to reverse side. Turn over.

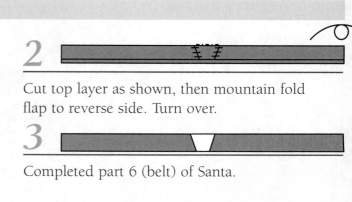

3
Completed part 6 (belt) of Santa.

Santa Claus

36

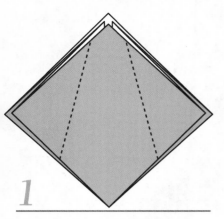

Part 7

1

Start with step 6 of Base Fold III. Valley fold.

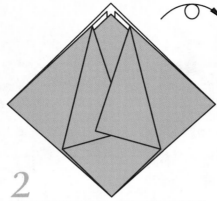

2

Apply glue, then turn over.

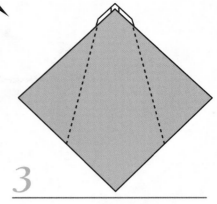

3

Valley folds and glue.

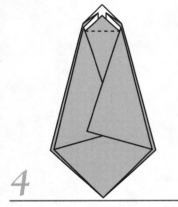

4

Valley folds both sides.

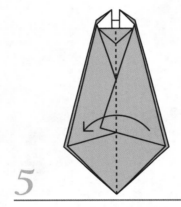

5

Valley folds both sides.

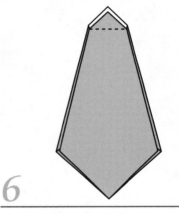

6

Valley folds both sides.

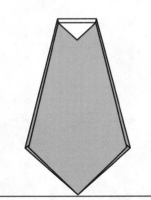

7

Push bottom upward and open top. (Open only one side when attaching to Santa.)

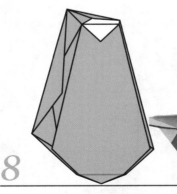

8

Completed part 7, Santa's toy sack.

Santa Claus

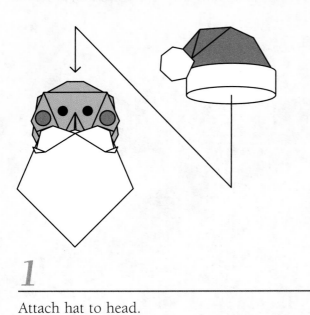

1

Attach hat to head.

2

Glue head part 2)
onto body (part 3)
and add belt
(part 6).

3

Glue sack (part 7)
onto shoulder, if
wanted. Attach
boots (part 5) to
legs (part 4)
and legs
to body, in
standing or
sitting position.

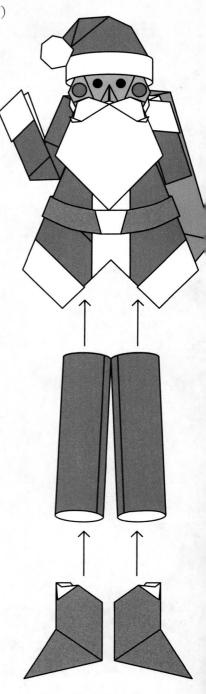

4

Completed Santa Claus standing…and sitting.

Reindeer

Part 1

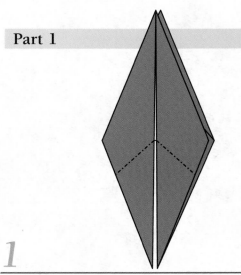

1

Start with Base Fold III. Inside reverse folds.

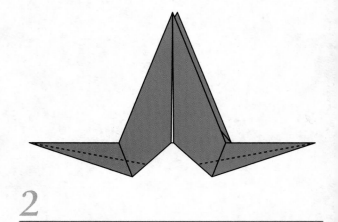

2

Valley folds both sides.

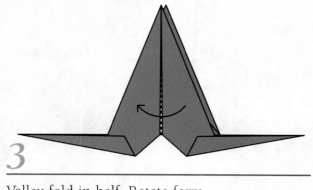

3

Valley fold in half. Rotate form.

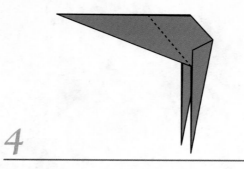

4

Outside reverse fold.

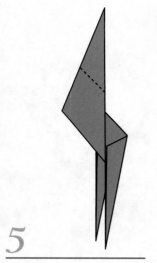

5

Outside reverse folds.

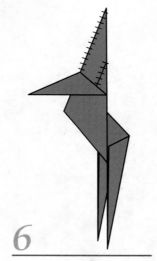

6

Make cuts as shown.

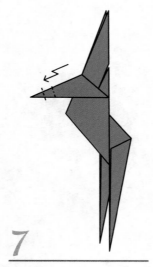

7

Pleat folds.

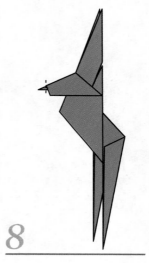

8

Outside reverse fold.

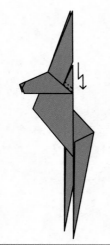

9

Pleat folds both sides.

10

Tuck ears in.

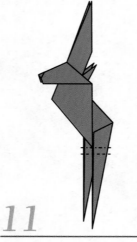

11

Pleat folds.

12

Pull and crimp fold.

Reindeer

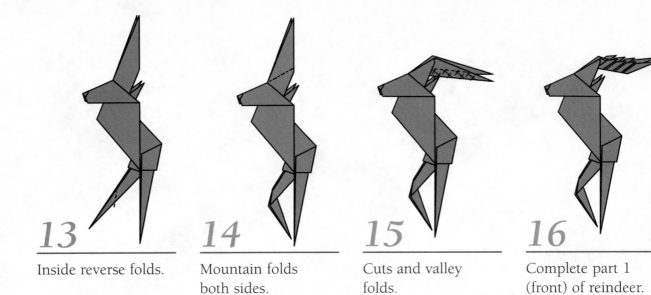

13
Inside reverse folds.

14
Mountain folds both sides.

15
Cuts and valley folds.

16
Complete part 1 (front) of reindeer.

Part 2

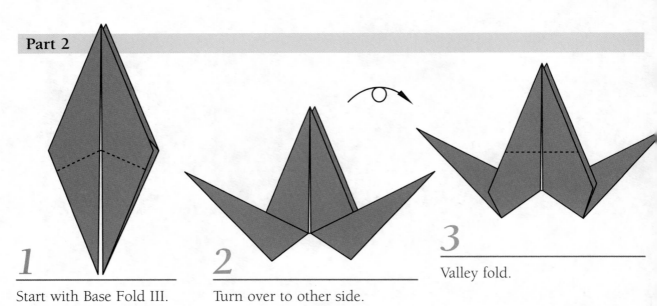

1
Start with Base Fold III. Valley folds.

2
Turn over to other side.

3
Valley fold.

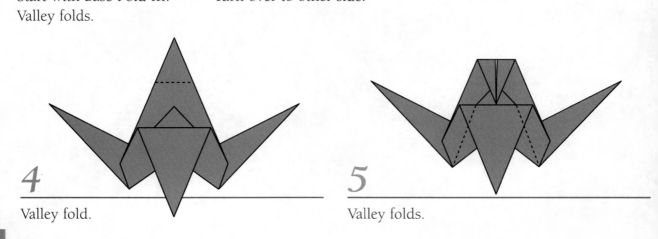

4
Valley fold.

5
Valley folds.

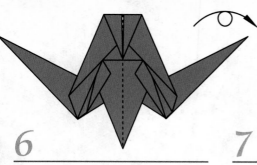

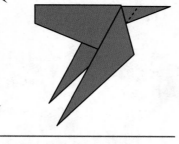

6

Fold in half, then rotate.

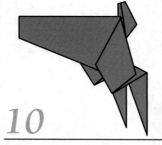

7

Outside reverse fold.

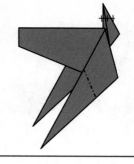

8

Inside reverse fold, both sides.

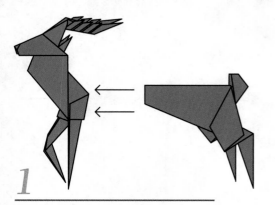

9

Inside reverse folds, both sides.

10

Completed part 2 (rear) of reindeer.

To Attach

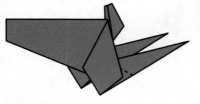

1

Join both parts together, and apply glue to hold.

2

Completed Reindeer.

Santa's Sleigh

Part 1

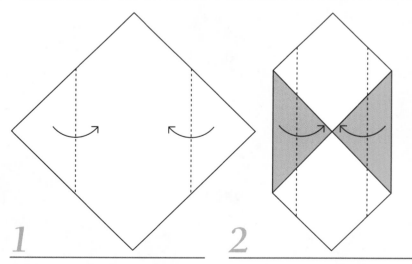

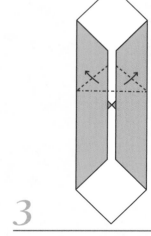

1 Valley folds to center.

2 Again, valley folds to center.

3 Valley/mountain folds to boxlike shape, glue to hold.

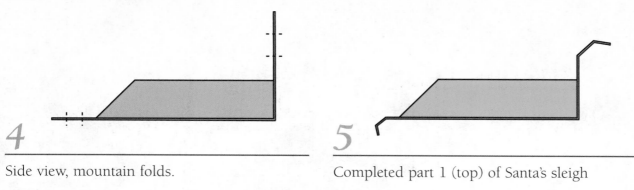

4

Side view, mountain folds.

5

Completed part 1 (top) of Santa's sleigh

Part 2

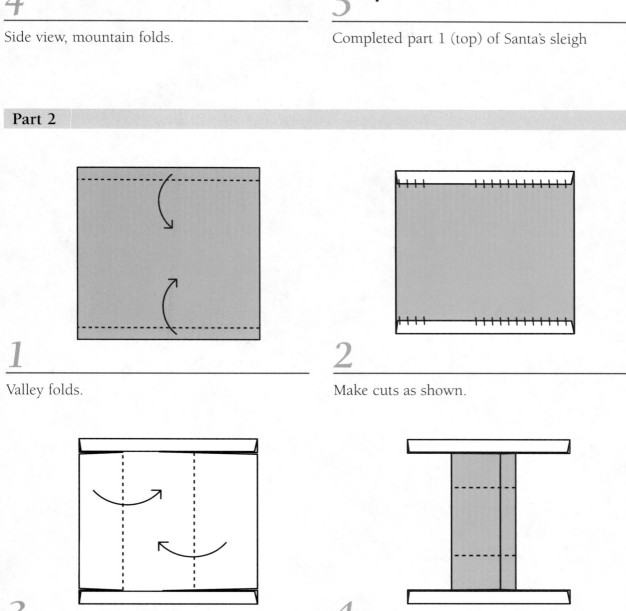

1

Valley folds.

2

Make cuts as shown.

3

Valley folds, right side then left.

4

Valley folds.

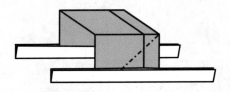

5

Mountain folds both sides.

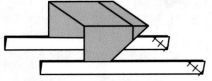

6

Make cuts as shown, and discard.

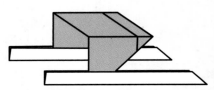

7

Completed part 2 (runners) of Santa's sleigh.

To Attach

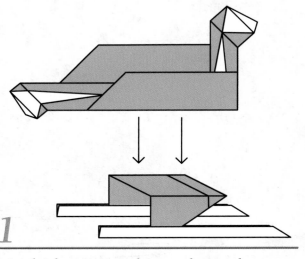

1

Join sleigh parts 1 and 2 together as shown and apply glue to hold.

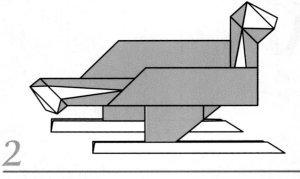

2

Completed Santa's Sleigh.

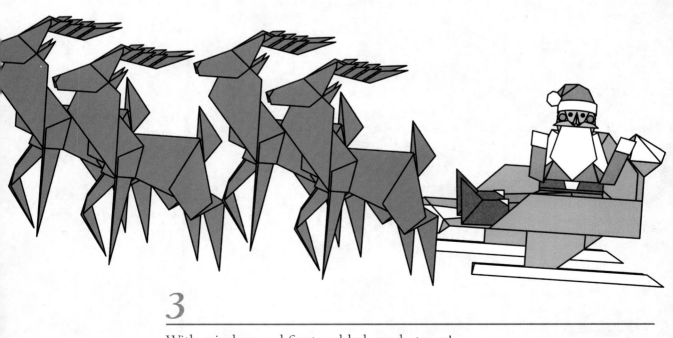

3

With reindeer and Santa added, ready to go!

ISBN 0-439-47410-8

12 11 10 9 8 7 6 5 4 3   3 4 5 6 7/0

Printed in the U.S.A.   09

First Scholastic printing, November 2002

Design by Judy Morgan
Edited by Claire Bazinet